T0151529

AWAKENINGS

POEMS OF
LIFE AND LOVE

KATHRYN CAROLE ELLISON

Published by Lady Bug Books, an imprint of Brisance Books Group.
Lady Bug Press and the distinctive ladybug logo are registered trademarks of
Lady Bug Books, LLC.

Lady Bug Books
400 112th Avenue N.E.
Suite 230
Bellevue, WA 98004
www.ladybugbooks.net

For information about custom editions, special sales and permissions, please contact
Brisance Books Group at specialsales@brisancebooksgroup.com

Manufactured in the United States of America
ISBN: 978-1-944194-23-9

First Edition: May 2017

A NOTE FROM THE AUTHOR

The poems in this book were written over many, many years...
as gifts, of sorts, to my children. I began writing them in the
1970s, when my children were reaching the age of reason and
as I found myself in the position of becoming a single parent.
I needed something special to share with them—something that
would become a tradition, a ritual they could always count on...

And so the Advent Poems began—one day, decades ago—
with a poem 'gifted' to them each day during the December
holiday season every year. Forty years later... my children still
look forward to the poems that started a family tradition
that new generations have come to cherish.

It's my sincere hope that you will embrace and enjoy them
as we have and share them with those you love.

Children of the Light was among the first poems I wrote and
is included in each of the *Poems of Life and Love* books in
The Ellison Collection: *Heartstrings, Inspirations, Celebrations,
Sojourns, Awakenings,* and *Sanctuary.* After writing hundreds
of poems, it is still my favorite. The words came from my
heart and my soul and flowed so effortlessly that it was
written in a single sitting. All I needed to do was
capture the words on paper.

Light, to me, represented all that was good and pure and right
with the world, and I believed then—as I do today—that those
elements live in my children... and perhaps in all of us.
We need only to dare...

– KCE

DEDICATION

To my parents: Herb and Bernice Haas

Mom, you were the poet who went before me...
unpublished, but appreciated nonetheless.

And Dad, you always believed in me,
no matter what direction my life took.
Thank you for your faith in me,
and for your unconditional love.

TABLE OF CONTENTS

LIFE'S JOYS

LIFE'S LESSONS

LIFE'S GIFTS

LIFE'S JOYS

Be open to epiphanies

When all is mostly said and done
You really are the only one
Who can, indeed, know when to change
Your views on things, to rearrange
Patterns which keep you in a rut
With no way out; a lost cause – but
Your work has only just begun.

Sometimes an epiphany, quite intact –
A realization of a significant fact
About your life and your direction –
Arises from a mere reflection;
Or else an event, quite commonplace,
Can bring you around, and face to face,
With your next significant act.

A view into your personality
Giving you a whole new way to see
Where you are and where you'll go –
What you believe and how you'll grow.
Such moments decide your charted course
Bringing you in touch with your inner source.
As your life evolves in harmony.

FORGIVENESS

Without forgiveness, there is anger.
Without forgiveness, there is bitterness.
Without forgiveness, there is hatred.
Are these three things with which you want to live?

So... somebody did something bad to you –
So... somebody said something bad about you,
And you were deeply wounded by it.
Do you want to carry that pain through life with you?

Forgiveness is a choice to free yourself from anger.
Forgiveness is a choice to free yourself from bitterness.
Forgiveness is a choice to free yourself from hatred.
It's not an easy choice, but a necessary one.

You don't have to forgive because they deserve it.
You don't have to forgive because they want it.
You don't have to forgive because someone told you to.
You forgive because you don't need the pain anymore.

CHILDREN OF THE LIGHT

There are those souls who bring the light,
Who spill it out for all to share,
And with a joy that does excite
They show the world that they do care.
It is so very bright.

In this sharing, love does pervade
Into their lives and cycles 'round;
And as this light is outward played
The love is also inward bound.
It is an awesome trade.

You are a soul whose light is shared.
It comes from deep within your heart.
It's best because it is not spared,
Because it's total, not just part.
And I am glad you've dared.

LIVING WITH PASSION

"A life without passion is no life at all."
You've heard these words before.
But reading or hearing is only one step
Toward grasping meaning, and furthermore,
Here are more words to support this proposal,
The truth of which I have no doubt.
"If you have no purpose, you have no passion.
And without passion you've sold yourself out."

If cynicism and apathy are regular moods
That endanger your daily routine,
It's because you've abandoned yourself and what matters,
And lost the truth of what might have been.

Passion, excitement and confidence are
Needed elements for everyday living.
They're necessary to your peace of mind,
And a joyous exchange you are giving.
When you are passionate the others around you
Feed off your amazing dance.
They absorb your bounce and give it right back,
And joy is not left to chance.

REALITY IS RELATIVE

Reality is only *your* slice of life.
It's not another's, that's for sure.
What is real to you, to someone else
May present as another picture.

And so it follows, does it not,
Your angle of perspective is such
That what you think is right for others
Doesn't amount to very much?

If you are to live and understand
Another person's view of things.
You must stretch you minds, open your hearts
And be aware of each other's feelings.

THE QUALITY OF LOVE

Taking things and people for granted
Can put you in an unhappy state,
And taking a relationship for granted
Is an insult to you and your mate.

Put the quality of your relationship first.
Put it even above your career.
A greeting, an awareness when they enter the room –
A decision to be of good cheer,

No assignment, no deadline, no project you might have
Is as important as the quality of your love.
For the joy your relationship brings to you…
On your knees, thank the heavens above.

TOUCH

I hear your words; I see your face;
I smell the raindrops in your hair.
The faint smell of the coffee you drank
Hangs lightly in the air.

You are inside you and experience me;
And from inside me I experience you.
We remain separate entities, and do not meet
Until, by magic, we do.

We shake hands, perhaps, or trade pats on the back;
We may even go so far as an embrace.
The magic of touch brings with it discovery
Of how our lives interlace.

Through simply touching, we transmit to each other
The power of life we each hold inside.
We discover the inner and outer dimensions
In which we both abide.

The outside... with its flesh and bone...
And the inside... where we have our being...
Come together in the dance of life.
It is all there for the seeing.

It's no wonder that the laying on of hands
Promotes healing in every way;
That just the touch of another human being
Can be enough to save the day.

LOVE

All of the arts of living, it seems,
Are merged in the spectrum of love.
Friendship, awareness, happiness – the good life –
Fit together like a hand in a glove.

Love is the foundation and the apex
Of the pyramid of our existence.
It expands the vision and opens the heart.
Its influence in our lives is immense.

Love's the upward thrust that lifts men to heights.
It's a dynamic motivation.
It's the creative fire, keeping our torches aflame.
For progress it's an inspiration.

Love penetrates the mysteries of life.
It's the dove of peace to be sure.
It is tenderness, compassion, forgiveness and tolerance.
It is all of our motives pure.

Love is the supreme good, yet it is down-to-earth,
And it reaches the outermost star.
It's the valley of humility and the mountaintop of ecstasy.
It is everything you are.

Love is the perfect antidote to fear –
It washes away negative feelings.
The art of love is God at work
Through you in all your dealings.

BE YOURSELF

Be an observer of all behavior
So that you can become more open
To more behavioral possibilities.

You will learn a great deal more
When you are open to everything.
Do not just aim to please the teacher.

Style can never replace what's true,
And simple wisdom holds its own
With knowing all specific facts.

Potency is acting from one's center,
Not from creating an impression of strength,
Even if others are willing to be fooled.

A down-to-earth person who is well centered
Can do the task at hand with ease
And be effective, not just busy.

Effective action arises out of
Silence and a clear sense of being,
And offers you a source of peace.

TRUST

You may lose occasionally in trusting too many,
But you'll lose more in trusting too few.
While a few prove false and you are disappointed,
Each person you meet deserves a fresh view.

It goes along with positive thinking...
The premise that most people are good;
That people generally want to be their best...
To behave just as they should.

Your trust that the world is evolving and turning
The way it's supposed to do
Tells me not so much about the world
As it tells me, darlings, about you.

The changes you introduce to your world as you live
Are exactly *your* right ones to make,
Because they will be wise and enhance your lives,
No matter the directions they take.

I trust you both to trust yourselves...
That's of foremost importance to you.
Then trust of others will follow in the wake,
And show up in everything you do.

THE SOURCE OF YOUR POWER

No matter the course your life will take,
There's one basic thing you'll need.
That is awareness of what is happening,
And *how* it happens, indeed.

If you have awareness, then you can act
According to your highest order.
Steering clear of trouble most every time,
You learn to avoid disorder.

Remember that you, also, are part of the same
Natural Order by which others are bound.
Your life unfolds along the same guidelines;
You are rooted in the common ground.

Being like everything else just means
That you are wonderfully ordinary.
But consciously knowing; or being aware;
Well, that's truly extraordinary!!

By knowing how this universality works
And acting accordingly, you tower.
It is the source of your endurance and good.
It is the source of your power.

TRUE FRIENDSHIP

Kind sentiment is nice, it sounds quite good
But sentiment alone is not enough.
Without kind deeds to support the words
The likelihood of true friendship is rough.

If you're lucky enough to have a friend
Whose words and actions correspond,
Then you are blessed because you have
A special unbreakable bond.

And if you are someone who returns in kind
This friendship of words and action
Then you're someone who is in great demand;
You've reached mutual satisfaction.

LIFE'S LESSONS

IDEAS AND ACTIONS

What is bread without butter, or sugar without cream?
What is yin without yang, or sleep without dream?
One fits with the other, of that I am sure –
Alone they're incomplete; together they endure.

An idea is incomplete when standing on it's own.
The other half is action, and of course it's been shown
That if ideas have no punch, or no vitality in them,
Then action cannot follow. There's a quirk in the system.

Deeds cannot exist in the vacuum of the mind.
Thoughts with action change all of humankind.
Ideas first for planning, then with action to be matched,
So all of this potential... can finally be unlatched.

CRITICISM

Criticism is something we encounter every day.
It's everywhere. We give and we take.
And sometimes, if applied in a palatable manner,
We can learn from our own mistakes.

Good can result from even one's loudest critic,
If one can stand their clatter.
Look well, my dears, for their nugget of truth.
That only, in your life, will matter.

If advice you receive only brings you comfort
You may need more critical eyes,
Your path to enlightenment comes in many forms.
Sometimes it wears a disguise.

ELDER WISDOM

Old Cherokee wisdom passed down to the young
Around a campfire burning bright...
The Elder Woman sharing her stories so wise
To a granddaughter basking in the light.

The subject was about a battle that rages...
(Couched in terms of two wolves in a fight)
The fight goes on inside people each day
Between Good and Evil – wrong and right.

Evil is anger. It's envy and jealousy.
It's sorrow and regret and greed;
On the other hand, Good is joy, peace and love.
It is hope and serenity, truths to heed.

The young girl turned to her grandmother and asked,
Her face in an earnest, questioning need...
'Which one wins?' she asked the Elder Woman.
The Old Woman's answer: 'The one you feed.'

HUMILITY

Humility is not thinking less of yourself.
It's simply thinking of yourself less.
Humility is not considered cowardice, either,
And meekness is not weakness.
Humility is the solid foundation of all virtues.
If you have it, you are indeed blessed!

True humility is intelligent self-respect
Which keeps us from thinking of ourselves as magnificent,
Or too meanly, as well – keeping it balanced.
Humility is simply a correct self-judgment.
It makes us modest by reminding us how far
We have come short of becoming excellent.

THE BASICS

Having... Doing... then Being –
It's like reciting your ABCs.
One step follows the other
As innately as you please.

The natural flow of learning
Is a three-step process, true.
How quickly you reach your goal
Depends, of course, on you.

First you start by **having**
The equipment that you need
To learn your chosen field
Before you can proceed.

You practice by **doing** the steps
(Maybe take some lessons for knowing).
You do it over and over, and
Your expertise is growing.

The last step is the **being**.
The practice time is well spent.
You perform easily without effort.
And being is transcendent.

HAVING

You can't have the butter without churning the cream;
Nor the kernel from the ear without husking the corn.
You can't blame others when you feel slighted.
Your task is *yours* from the moment you are born.

Quitting too soon before reaching the goal
Is the most common deterrence from reaching success.
An inadequate search is certain to bring
Second-rate victories – certainly less
Than what you will gain if you ride to the end
And pursue the goal till there's no more to do.
Having requires striving, there's no other way;
But that is something you already knew.

Nobody owes you anything at all
Except respect when it has been earned.
'Free rides' aren't free, no matter what we think.
Someone will nearly always get burned.

It always feels right when you've stayed on the trail.
You gain self-respect – the very best feeling.
The thought, sweat and patience that's brought the success
Send all the negatives of the experience reeling.
So, don't quit too soon if you want, for your life,
The best that the world has for you in store.
Go for the gusto, take a chance, jump right in.
My darlings, it's there; just open *your* door.

LAUGHTER IS GOOD MEDICINE

Laughter is good medicine.
It is the very best, it's said.
It lifts your spirits to the skies,
And brings to you some peace instead.

The doctors now, and the scientists
Are doing research on the subject of mirth.
They've found results most interesting:
They report to us what we've known since birth.

Laughter gets rid of those negative hormones,
Like cortisol, adrenaline and dopamine.
It increases the good ones, like your endorphins.
It's a way for you to let off steam.

It provides for you a noticeable release,
Helping you physically and mentally, it seems.
It even provides a workout for your heart,
And probably even gives you wonderful dreams.

It can be used to lighten a moment
When anger, stress, or negative emotions
Seem to block your path to understanding
When you're in the middle of knotty commotions.

Laughter gives you perspective when you're stressed
By an event or a thought, or even fear.
And when you laugh it eases the burden
Of those around you. It's perfectly clear:

If you but look for humor where
They say it isn't, and then share
A bit of levity. Oh my –
The good things only multiply.

HIGHEST AND BEST USE

Imagine the tragedy if you had not been born
In the time and the place that you were.
The world as we know it would not be the same.
Everywhere you go you bring pleasure.

Chance plays a part, or so it seems,
In the way you play out your lives.
Meeting someone here, an adjustment there –
That's how your development thrives!

You need to know your 'highest and best' use
In this world in order to excel;
Then pursue it with every fiber of your being.
Be in charge, and your doubts will dispel.

Each of us is blessed with a particular gift –
At least one, and most likely more;
A gift given at birth by a Higher Power
To identify, to cherish, and furthermore,
You must exercise that gift to better yourselves
And those whom you hold dear.
You'll find the purpose for which you're meant
And you'll practice it every day of the year.

Imagine if Einstein had lived his life
As a truck driver or a merchant or a sailor;
Or if Mother Teresa had worked as a waitress,
Or an accountant or a model or a tailor!

It boggles the mind to think of people
In jobs for which they're unsuited –
Jobs that threaten their total health;
Jobs thought to be safe when pursued.

You may already be in your own right field,
Or you might just be treading water;
But when you know your own 'highest and best' use,
Pursue it! Your bliss will be greater!

LISTENING

The key to the art of listening, my loves,
Is selectivity, it has been said.
You alone stand guard and decide
What you'll allow into your head.

Listen to the good; tune your ears to love –
To hope and courage, to self-esteem.
Tune out gossip and fear and resentment.
You decide for yourself your own theme.

Listen to the beautiful! Relax with the music,
Which inspires mankind to do good.
And listen to nature's cacophony of sounds,
Including your own, if you would.

Listen with your eyes. Let your imagination soar,
As you read poetry and novels by the pound!
As you stroll through a gallery of paintings
Let your own soaring mind provide sound.

Be discerning, seek truth with an open mind,
And listen patiently, not in a hurry.
Listen for essence, and learn as you go;
Listen with your heart, not your ˙jury.˙

Listen to yourself, to your noblest impulses,
To the deepest and highest you can reach.
Be still and meditate; listen with intuition
For the inspiring wisdom there to teach.

CONTROL

The desire for happiness and freedom prevails.
To find it one must look to one's personal details.
If you have to be 'in the know' on every little thing,
Chances are you'll miss grabbing the proverbial 'brass ring.'

Some things are within our control; some are not.
And here is where the poet thickens the plot:
Within our control are our own opinions;
Aspirations and desires? Also in our dominions.

These things are subject to our influence directly:
We can control our inner lives, if done correctly.
We always have choices about our own inner lives.
The content and the character are our inner drives.

Outside our control are things not of our concern;
Things beyond control and with experience we'll learn:
Body type, societal status, whether we're born poor or rich.
All external, all beyond our ability to switch.

There's a tendency among people to think they can control
The activities of others... in fact, it becomes their goal.
Things outside our power are weak and dependent
Upon the whims of others... can cause resentments.

If you attempt to adopt the affairs of others...
Even your mother's, your sister's, or brother's...
Your pursuits will be thwarted and you will become
A fault-finding, anxious, and unhappy person.

Know what you can control and what you cannot.
And happiness and freedom will be yours on the spot.
It's a simple principle by which to live.
If followed closely, you'll get more than you give.

LIFE IS SHORT

You've heard the expression, 'Life is short!'
For some it can be short, indeed.
Learn to make your every action count.
You need loving patience to succeed.

Patience must begin first with yourself,
Then it radiates outward from there.
As your day unfolds, and your tasks get done,
You'll find a peacefulness you can share.

Some loving words, or a giant hug
You'd give – or maybe a soulful glance.
Make every act count each day you live.
You might not get a second chance.

LIFE'S GIFTS

HOPE

Hope is being able to see that there is light,
Despite all of the darkness that may surround.
Learn from yesterday, hope for today, and for tomorrow.
It's a formula for living most profound.

You must never deprive anyone of hope...
To live without hope is hardly living at all.
It may be all some people have left in their lives.
Life with hope is best overall.

Hope is like peace... not a gift from above.
It's a gift only we can give one another.
Hope is like the sun that, as you journey toward it,
Casts the shadow of your burdens asunder.

Capacity for hope endows a sense of destination,
And also the energy to get started.
Let your hopes, not your hurts, shape your future.
Listen closely to wisdom as it is imparted.

WIT

It's when the going gets tough that the tough get silly;
Laughter is a very good way to survive.
When people around you wear a grimace, not a smile,
You begin to wonder if they're even alive.

Society may insist that you conform to its rules
In every little thing you say, think, or do.
But wit is a safety valve for any constraint.
You can bid the seriousness a firm 'Adieu!'

It's amazing, in the face of all the old restrictions
That society feels it needs to impose,
An individual always finds a way to bypass them
Without having to voice his intention to oppose.

The more the freedoms tighten, the more repressed you feel,
And there exists a greater need for wit.
Keep smiling, have fun as you live your life.
Laughter will always fill your day… I submit.

FAMILIARITY

"Why does the snake not bite the attorney?"
(A joke you've heard many times...)
"Because of professional courtesy."
(Oh, how I struggle with rhymes!)

There's a thread of logic in the above-mentioned tale
(Here's where you listen attentively...)
"Those who practice the same profession
Recognize each other instinctively." *

Not only that, but "those who practice
The same vices..." are also in kinship.
They spot each other across the room.
They seek each other's companionship.

Like attracts like, or so it seems –
A profession, a vice or a value.
So look at the qualities of those you're around,
And know that they're ever so true.

 * Marcel Proust (1871–1922) | French Novelist

REPUTATION

The way to gain a good reputation
Is to be what you desire to appear.
It takes twenty years to build a reputation,
But only five minutes to let it disappear.

You can build a reputation on what you're 'going' to do.
Work is the price you pay to achieve it.
Build your reputation by helping others achieve theirs.
You both reap the riches, you both get the benefit.

Your reputation is in the hands of others:
This fact you probably have already discovered.
But you have complete control of your character...
It's much easier kept than recovered.

Character is what you are all day long,
And reputation is what others think you are.
Everywhere you go, you're the second to arrive:
Your reputation precedes you. (You're a star!)

If you take care of your character, my friends,
Your reputation will be fine, I suspect.
A word to the wise: Don't pay attention to someone
Who has not earned your complete respect.

CONFIDENCE

Confidence is contagious, but so is it's lack;
If you don't think you can, you won't!
Confidence isn't optimism, or a character attribute.
It's the expectation of a positive outcome up front.

Confidence, once described by a motivational speaker,
Is going after Moby Dick in a rowboat,
And taking the tartar sauce along with you.
It's 'Fish and Chips for All' – you will promote.

Love who you are! Embrace who you are!
It's confidence and self-esteem you are showing.
With confidence you have won even before you started.
You must still run the race, but your energy is flowing.

Action breeds confidence and courage that is measurable.
When you have confidence, you have a lot of fun!
And when you have fun, you can do amazing things!
Get going! Your work has only just begun.

You can buy all the trappings to look the part.
You can dress up in sartorial magnificence.
But remember this as you look in the mirror:
The most beautiful thing you can wear is confidence.

NO SHAME, NO BLAME

If it is our *feelings* about things that torment us,
Rather than the things themselves,
Then it follows that blaming others for this,
Is giving more energy than the thing deserves.

Things themselves don't hurt or hinder us,
And nor do other people.
It's how we view – and then react –
That gives us the biggest trouble.

Placing blame on others, or even ourselves
In situations of misfortune
Is seeking the 'easy explanation'
For events unbidden or inopportune.

One of the signs of the moral progress
Is the gradual obliteration of blame.
We see the futility of pointing a finger
At another, or at the one with your name.

Things simply are what they are... no more!
And other people will think what they think.
It is not an inkling of concern to us.
No shame, No blame... make the link.

PHOENIX RISES

'Fire is the test of gold,' it is said;
'Adversity, of strong men.'
Seneca of distant pre–Christ days
Wrote those wise words with his pen.

Look at each misfortune you endure.
Study it carefully and seek to find
The fringe benefits – the lessons to learn.
Good from every setback can be mined.

There's a story of a miller, a grinder of grain,
Dependent upon the stream for his power.
A flood came along and washed away
His mill and all of his flour.

He lamented long hours, he cried up a storm,
Saying, "How could God do this to me?"
He felt helpless and hopeless as he stood on the site
Of what had once been his prosperity.

As his tears became dry and his eyes were clear
He looked around his former stronghold.
And glimmering there at the bank of the stream
Was a large deposit of gold.

That which impoverished him made him rich.
His plight (the flood) did reveal
What was there all the time, but covered up.
It took misfortune to make it real.

PROGRESS

Progress is that art that man must practice
In order that his conditions improve.
In every aspect of life, it seems,
One observes him on the move.

Held back by tyrants, ignorance and fear –
Economic disasters and war –
He breaks the shackles and marches ahead
To where he has not been before.

His buildings evolve from caves right on up
To high-rise and steel cantilever.
He uses free time to improve his mind,
Plugging his modem into the receiver.

Future transportation systems may have us airborne
From our own garages to Mars.
But in the meantime our world's differences shrink
As we gain perspective from other stars.

Man has been delayed by ten thousand detours,
And yet rises after each fall.
He builds stronger and higher the things he's destroyed,
And always gives his all.

CONVICTION

The repetition of affirmations is what leads to belief,
And when belief becomes a deep conviction, things begin to happen.
That constant repetition is what carries your convictions,
And when you truly believe something, people will listen!

Conviction without experience often makes for harshness.
It's how you communicate it that drives the idea home.
Logic is the technique for adding conviction to truth.
You'll find that to be true, wherever you may roam.

You must stick to your convictions. They're yours and yours alone,
And you will abandon your assumptions when they no longer apply.
Convictions are believed to be the conscience of the mind.
Be true to them; be honest. Your sense of ease will multiply!

The word "no" that is uttered from your deepest conviction
Is better than a "yes" that is uttered to merely please.
It's dishonest to agree if you really don't believe,
But people often do. It's one of many life's absurdities.

A parting thought to you before this poem goes away...
It's a reminder to you that has the intention to instruct:
You can talk and argue, you can rant all you want,
But conviction is worthless unless it is converted into conduct.

MIRRORS

'What goes around, comes around,' so it's said.
'What we put out, we get back ten-fold.'
Cliches like these, and many others
Can tend to get 'rather old.'

There's an element of truth in these old sayings,
And lessons to be learned day by day.
The world mirrors back your wisdom or folly.
It's unavoidable – here it comes! – headed your way.

If your world's unmanageable or hard to bear;
If you don't like what you see around you,
Ask the question, 'How can I change myself ?'
And the answers will come flowing through.

'Cause change happens only when you decide
To take responsibility and make a move
Towards resolution; not staying in the problem.
When you change, your life will greatly improve.

YOU ARE WONDERFUL

As you learn to see others' shortcomings with wit
You'll be able to face your own,
And work to change and improve and grow...
And for hurts you've inflicted, atone.

Remember this, it's your mind that makes
Your faults so big or so small.
Your imagination can create a monster size
Or one that's not very big at all.

Good humor helps when you work on you.
It makes your job easier by far.
It helps you see for yourself just how
Wonderful you really are.

SELF AWARENESS

You are not your feelings, you are not your thoughts,
And you are not even your various moods.
The fact that you can even think about things
Sets you apart from the animals in the woods.

Be aware of yourself, it allows you to see
From a clearer perspective all around.
It affects your attitude and behavior as well,
In ways bordering on the profound.

It allows you to see yourself, of course;
And others, from their perspective.
It maps the basic nature of all mankind...
Gives understanding that is more objective.

Self-awareness leads you down remarkable paths.
It's a lifelong process, to be sure.
It enhances your lives in immeasurable ways,
Opening communication lines so pure.

A CLOSING THOUGHT

POETRY

It's the revelation
Of a sensation
That the poet
(Wouldn't you know it)
Believes to be
Felt only interiorly
And personal to
The writer who
... writes it.

It's the interpretation
Of a sensation
That was fueled by
A poet's sigh
And believed to be
Shared mutually
And personal to
The lucky one who
... reads it.

About the Author

Kathryn Carole Ellison is a former newspaper columnist
and journalist and, of course, a poet.

She lives near her children and stepchildren and their families in the
Pacific Northwest, and spends winters in the sunshine of Arizona.

You might find her on the golf course with friends, river rafting,
writing poems... or at the opera.

Late bloomer

Our culture honors youth with all
It's unbridled effervescence.
We older ones sit back and nod
As if in acquiescence.

And when our confidence really gels
In early convalescence...
'We can't be getting old!' we cry,
'We're still struggling with adolescence!'

Acknowledgments

I have many people to thank...

First of all, my children Jon and Nicole LaFollette, for inspiring the writing of these poems in the first place. And for encouraging me to continue my writing, even though their wisdom and compassion surpass mine.

My wonderful stepchildren, Debbie and John Bacon, Jeff and Sandy Ellison, and Tom and Sue Ellison, who, with their children and grandchildren, continue to be a major part of my life and are loved deeply by me. These poems are for you, too.

Eva LaFollette, the dearest daughter-in-law one could ever wish for... and one of my dearest friends. Your encouragement and interest are so appreciated.

My good friends who have received a poem or two of mine in their Christmas cards these many years, for complimenting me on the messages in my poems. Your encouragement kept me writing.

To Kim Kiyosaki who introduced me to the right person to get the publishing process underway... that person being Mona Gambetta with Brisance Books Group who has the experience and know-how to make these books happen.

And finally, to John Laughlin, a fellow traveler in life, who encourages me every day in the writing and publishing process. John, I love having you in my cheering section!

OTHER BOOKS
by Kathryn Carole Ellison

SOJOURNS

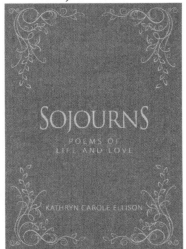

SANCTUARY

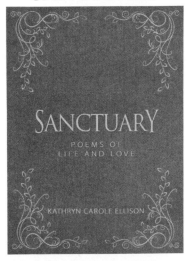

HEARTSTRINGS

INSPIRATIONS

CELEBRATIONS